Corporate

Accounting

(How) Can Companies Tell the Truth?

Richard Evans

Consultant in Social and Ethical Accounting

GROVE BOOKS LIMITED
RIDLEY HALL RD CAMBRIDGE CB3 9HU

Contents

First Impression January 2001
ISSN 1470-854X
ISBN 1 85174 453 3

1

The Business of Business and Society

'Shell to come clean and go green'
'BT won over by argument for ethical audit'
'Corporations call in ethics police'

When headlines like these appeared in the daily press in the mid-1990s they were greeted with a certain scepticism. Were these declarations anything more than a new corporate public relations stunt? A few years on, increasing numbers of large business corporations are publishing or preparing to publish detailed, and often independently verified, reports on their impact on society. If you want to see how some leading companies are shaping up to their newly discovered responsibilities, you will find a list of published social and ethical reports, and the web-sites where you can view them, in the Appendix.

The aim of the booklet is to increase awareness and understanding of this significant trend in international business by describing the developing phenomenon of social accounting. Business is probably the single most important influence on Western culture. It controls more wealth than governments and shapes our lives and our futures more powerfully than politics or religion. We are all involved in business and as Christians we have a responsibility to shape our involvement in the light of the gospel. I hope this booklet will encourage you to support the businesses that are trying to be honest and to listen to, and be accountable to, society.

The business of business is no longer purely 'business' but involves satisfying the needs of our global society today in ways which will not damage the lives and potential of future generations. As people who take our responsibilities for creation and other people seriously, we need to understand the trend and learn how we can play our role as stakeholders in business and society.

Social accounting and reporting has developed as a pragmatic response to increasing consumer awareness and concern with the behaviour of large companies. However, the practice has developed in advance of any coherent theoretical basis. In tracing its origins I will outline several different theories that underlie social accountability reporting and some theological reflections of my own.

Business Ethics and Changes in Society [1]

In 1989 Dr Jose Maria Basagoiti, addressing the Second Symposium on Enterprise and Humanism, said, 'The social role of the business world is an economic role. Society needs the well functioning of the economy, and that is the social role

---

1 Some of this material first appeared in a paper by the author, 'Business Ethics and Changes in Society,' in the *Journal of Business Ethics* 10, (1991) pp 871–876.

entrusted to businessmen.'

While there is a deal of truth in the statement there are also assumptions that need to be questioned. If the term 'economy' is taken in its narrow sense as the generation and management of wealth, this looks like another, somewhat milder, version of Milton Friedman's famous dictum, 'Few trends could so thoroughly undermine the very foundation of our free society as the acceptance by corporate officials of a social responsibility other than to make as much money for their shareholders as possible.'[2]

Few businesses today would openly subscribe to such a view. On the contrary, many would say that while economic success is fundamental, businesses acknowledge a wide range of responsibilities to the environment and society. In practice, however, few would accept that they should be equally accountable to society for these broader responsibilities, as they are to shareholders for their economic performance. Globalisation of the capital market has increased the pressure on financial bottom line performance. Consequently, many find they have to devote a disproportionate amount of resources to pursuing or avoiding take-overs and other threats to their survival, forced on them by dissatisfied shareholders.

The other problem is the notion of *the business world*, as if this were a separate universe of values and goals distinct from society at large. Businesses are not distinct social entities; they are part of the collage of human activities we describe as society.

The Impact of Business

It is far too reductionist an analysis to describe the social role of business as a purely economic role. Business often creates and always influences the physical and biological environment society inhabits. Business plays a major role in human development both through the way people at work are enabled to fulfil their economic role in society, and through its effects on those whom it excludes from an economic role through the strategies of mechanisation, downsizing and redundancy. Marketing has a huge impact on social culture by shaping and influencing the intensity of peoples' wants and needs, with resulting changes in lifestyle within society and consequential impacts on the environment.

Today, most powerful and many smaller businesses are multinational in their ownership, employment, supply chains, the distribution of their goods and services, and the environmental impact of their emissions and by-products. 'Dirty industries' are exported to third-world countries where environmental regulation may be inadequate. Most of our clothing is now made in countries with extremely low wages and poor protection for workers. Our food retailers are heavily dependent on agriculture in tropical countries where low commodity prices, social disruption and environmental and health impacts are damaging the lives of millions. Economic growth fuelled by over-consumption in the industrialized countries has consistently resulted in starvation, economic insecurity and the de-

2   M Friedman, *Capitalism and Freedom* (Chicago: University of Chicago Press, 1962).

pletion of natural resources in the third world.

However, while challenging any residual notion that business should be left alone to get on with what it does best, we should not demonize all business because of the sins of our fathers and the widespread abuses that persist today. Some businesses are trying very hard to take a more holistic view of their role and their relationship to society. Two ideas are driving the change: the idea of the *stakeholder* and the recognition of *corporate accountability*.

Stakeholding

Whether or not we own shares, we are all stakeholders in a surprisingly large number of businesses. We all have an investment in business, as consumers, suppliers, employees, through our pension providers, banks, ISA's and shares, and as members of the community.

Money is not the only capital in a capitalist economy. There is some justification for saying that it is the least important and only a proxy for the real capital that drives our economic system: social capital and ecological capital. Economics is no more or less than the process through which humans create social and environmental outcomes. All of us are investing social capital in business, in the form of our labour and intellect as employees and our contribution to education, science and technology research, social welfare systems and the political process as members of a democratic society. We also use up social capital through the impact our lifestyle and consumption has on the lives of people involved in the supply chain. And it is hard to imagine any manufactured product or business service that does not require the investment or expenditure of some environmental capital, and that is the capital on which life now, and in the future, depends. These ideas of *eco-justice* and *eco-efficiency* [3] define what we mean by sustainability. 'Sustainability is a commitment to satisfying lives for all within the means of nature.' [4]

Accountability

With the breakdown of 'authority' as a foundation for social cohesion, we are much more interested in how people and institutions in positions of power and responsibility discharge the *licence to operate* we give them through the ballot box and as consumers of their services and products. *Accountability* is the duty of an individual or organization to inform, explain and justify their actions—to provide an account—to those who are affected by them. The combination of these two ideas in social and ethical accounting, auditing and reporting make a powerful tool for changing business's impact on society.

Although the business activity of society involves many people, its control is in the hands of very few. This remains true in Britain in spite of the Government's

---

3   R Gray, D Owen, C Adams, *Accounting and Accountability* (London: Prentice Hall, 1996) pp 61, 223–226.
4   Title of a paper written for the Global Reporting Initiative (January 2000) by Paul Hawken and Mathis Wackernagel.

public floatations of state industries in the 1990s and the growth of equity-based savings and mortgages and private share ownership. Most businesses are still controlled by a small number of very large, institutional shareholders and by the managers. Consequently, the objectives of business have been easily diverted towards the interests of these minorities, such as the maximization of profit for the owners or the personal wealth and security of the top managers. Little regard is paid to the interests of the majority in society, who have little or no financial stake in the enterprise. However, things are changing, and Tony Blair's unveiling of 'the stakeholder society' has helped people think.

Stakeholders are people who have an explicit contract with the business, such as customers, suppliers and employees, or an implied contract, such as the duty of care for the environment or economic, health and safety responsibilities to the community. All categories of stakeholder invest money, or time, or intellect or their local amenity in the business and are entitled to a reasonable expectation that the business will exercise stewardship and make a return on their investment.

Stakeholding in business has been little affected by changes in ownership of shares, but much more by consumer awareness of corporate behaviour. The huge growth in private Internet access, consumer boycotts of companies and products and the introduction of new European Community legislation have all helped us to understand stakeholding.

Social and Ethical Accounting, Auditing and Reporting

Social and ethical accounting, auditing and reporting (SEAAR) is a systematic process for monitoring and reporting to all stakeholders the use that an organization makes of social and environmental capital and the impact it has on its stakeholders. At the heart of the process is the involvement of the organization's stakeholders in determining which aspects of performance affect their interests and should therefore be monitored and reported. The original SEAAR methodology was developed at Traidcraft plc, which published the first independently audited corporate social accounts in 1993. This is described in the next chapter.

The methodology and practice of SEAAR developed in advance of any clear theoretical agenda. The approaches adopted by Traidcraft were driven by concerns for *emancipation* and *inclusion* respectively.

What I have termed the *emancipation* theory is based on an extension of financial accounting ideas. Just as managers of a business give an account of their stewardship of the owners' (shareholders') financial investment, social accounting includes all stakeholders in the accounting process, with their different types of investment.

The *inclusion* theory is based on the idea of the business as a social construct—a partnership of discourse and activity—involving many categories of participants, or stakeholders, in achieving consensual goals within the constraints of negotiated conditions.

In addition to these two approahces, as the practice has evolved a strong

6

managerialist approach has emerged. Rather than a deliberate attempt to develop a coherent theoretical basis for the practice, its use has been identified in academic critiques of some social accounts.

My own perspective, described under the heading *accountability and complexity*, draws on the insights of all three of these approaches but attempts to establish a fourth approach using a more coherent theoretical basis. It recognizes the importance of uncertainty and the underlying interconnectedness of events rediscovered in the science of complexity.

These four approaches will be discussed in chapter three, which will also include my personal reflections on theological resonances I see in the theories underlying corporate social and ethical accountability and in the experience of doing it.

Christians have a particular responsibility to society and creation in their obligation to incarnate God's laws and to love their neighbour. There is nothing in Scripture to indicate that this obligation excludes business activity. In the academic literature on corporate responsibility the dominant view was, until the mid-1980s, that a corporate body could not have moral responsibility. The arguments have been well rehearsed in Justin Webley's, *Can Companies Sin?* (Grove Ethics booklet E 85).[5]

We also believe that God's laws and the cultural mandate are universal and provide rules and principles of behaviour for humankind as a whole. Accountability has a particular resonance with the biblical ideas of repentance and grace. Traidcraft's corporate social reporting was informed by its biblically based *Foundation Principles* and commitment to justice for the poor and marginalized. It is clear, even from the recent history of multinational companies like Union Carbide, Nestlé, Shell, Nike and many more, that issues of social justice and human rights are as alive today as they were in the time of the Prophet Amos:

Yahweh says this:
> 'For the three crimes, the four crimes of Israel, I have made my decree and will not relent: because they have sold the upright for silver and the poor for a pair of sandals, because they have crushed the heads of the weak into the dust and thrust the rights of the oppressed to one side...'

(Amos 2.6)

---

5   See also M G Valasquez, 'Why Corporations are Not Morally Responsible for Anything They Do' in J R Desjardins and J J McCall, *Contemporary Issues in Business Ethics* (Wadsworth, 1985).

2
Corporations Call in the Ethics Police

The chapter title is from an article in *The Independent on Sunday* in 1994 about Traidcraft's challenge to corporations to take up social accounting. The chapter describes how the process developed at Traidcraft.

Traidcraft Plc

Traidcraft had its origins in the recognition that something was profoundly wrong with our world. In the 1960s and 1970s the usual responses to the problem of endemic poverty in the third world attempted to treat the symptoms of poverty, rather than tackle the causes. They were about relief and welfare, not about fairness or justice.

To eradicate the poverty of millions of people in the South, businesses and consumers in the North would have to behave differently. The idea was simple enough. If small farmers and artisans in Asia, Africa and Latin America were paid fair prices and were allowed to sell their products freely to the rich markets in the North, international trade could directly benefit their families and communities, instead of being a cause of exploitation and poverty. Amartya Sen says poverty is not about what people do not have but about what they cannot do.[6]

Traidcraft was incorporated in 1979 and became a public limited company in 1984. It has a turnover of around £7.5 million from importing and marketing a range of food and handmade products from more than 100 small businesses and farmers co-operatives in twenty-six countries in Africa, Asia and Latin America.

Traidcraft described itself as a community of purpose, and the community is surprisingly large and geographically dispersed. It employs around 120 people, has 4,000 individual shareholders and around 4,500 people all over the UK belong to Traidcraft's Fair Traders' Scheme. They sell its products in their shops, homes, schools, churches, village halls, community centres and markets. Traidcraft also sells through its own mail order catalogues and in supermarkets.

Trading for Profit or Profit for Trading

Traidcraft's articles of association contain a set of Foundation Principles, which include 'promoting love and justice in international trade' and 'a commitment to practical service and partnership for change, which puts people before profit.' However, it is not a development charity. It is a business that will only survive if it trades profitably. It has to demonstrate that social goals and commercial viability are compatible. While Traidcraft is not at the cutting edge of twentieth-century technology, nor a model of free market enterprise, it is revolutionary.

Its founders rejected the Keynesian law of the free market in favour of the law

---

6 Amartya Sen, *Development as Freedom* (Oxford University Press, 1999).

of love and justice found in the Judaeo-Christian tradition. They also rejected the classical definition of the purpose of business—making its shareholders rich. This business' *raison d'être* was to improve market opportunities for small producers in the third world while ensuring, somehow, that everyone involved in Traidcraft was fairly rewarded for their contribution to its growth and prosperity.

For many years the company traded under the slogan: *Putting People before Profit*. While recognizing that profit was necessary to make the business grow, it did not define its purpose. For Traidcraft profit was far too abstract a summary of the outcome of the business processes. It did not tell the real life story of how the company treats people, whether they are valued or exploited. Neither does it show whether the company is achieving its mission of fighting poverty through trade and expanding the UK market for fairly traded products.

For most businesses the only stakeholder to whom the managers and directors are accountable has been the shareholder. Traidcraft's first share issue in 1984 sought to revive the original idea of equity as a share in the mission or purpose of the company and the accompanying risks. But it also broke the tradition that the shareholders' interests preceded all others. James Erlichman wrote in *The Guardian*, 'Traidcraft urgently needs a £300,000 cash injection from new shareholders—but it is offering them in return only "love, justice and equity." And equity to Traidcraft means putting a higher value on sharing the world's resources fairly than on its own share certificates. Investors must prefer goodness to greed and should never expect "personal gain or profit," the prospectus warns.'

The subordination of shareholders' interests to those of the partner enterprises in the developing countries was already well established. But how were the partners' interests, and those of employees, customers and the community to be represented when policy was being formed? The trustees of the Traidcraft Foundation, who hold the voting shares in the company, asked the directors to develop a process of accounting for the company's social impact and to carry out an annual audit of its performance against non-financial criteria. The managers were to report back to the Trustees who were responsible constitutionally for Traidcraft's Foundation Principles and particularly for its producers. Early in 1992 the Board agreed to publish its first externally audited account, at the same time as its annual statutory accounts, the following year.

The Idea of a Social Account of the Business

The terms 'social audit' and 'social accounts' seemed to be there right at the beginning of the discussion and undoubtedly owed their place in the business ethics vocabulary to the work of Charles Medawar and Social Audit Ltd in the 1970s. We also learned a lot about corporate social reporting from Traidcraft's first managing director, Richard Adams, who left Traidcraft in 1989 to set up a consumer research organization dealing with corporate ethics.[7]

---

7   R Adams, J Carruthers and S Hamil, *Changing Corporate Values: A Guide to Social and Environmental Policy and Practice in Britain's Top Companies* (London: Kogan Page, 1991).

Traidcraft's approach would differ from what we knew of the existing practice of external audits and corporate social reporting in a number of ways:

- It would be a system of voluntary reporting by the company itself.
- The accounts would record stakeholders' qualitative perceptions of the company's behaviour, with no attempt to reduce social impacts to a financial bottom line.
- It would acknowledge the legitimacy of stakeholders' different perspectives.
- All aspects of the business were up for scrutiny, not just the safe areas selected by the management or directors.
- Stakeholders would be asked to identify what aspects of performance were important to them and how they should be measured and reported.
- The report was to be produced annually rather than *ad hoc*.
- The social accounts report should be independently verified by an external auditor.

Developing a Methodology

The author and Simon Zadek, of the New Economics Foundation, published a 64-page booklet in April 1993, *Auditing the Market—A Practical Approach to Social Auditing*. The booklet came out before Traidcraft started compiling its first social accounts. Its preface said, 'It is our intention that the process we have engaged in here will result in a methodology and approach that can be applied to any business to audit its social and ethical performance, and that such "social audits" will become a significant indicator of success in the business world of the 21st Century.'

Key Elements of the Methodology
1. The Scope of the Account
The accounting 'entity' is defined, whether it is the whole company, specific business units within the whole company, specific production sites or geographical regions.

2. Establishing the Value Base
What are the social objectives and the ethical values against which the business's activities are to be assessed?

3. Defining the Stakeholders
Who are the key groups of people who can influence or are significantly affected by the activities of the business?

4. Establishing Social Performance Indicators
The principle of stakeholder evaluation requires stakeholder participation in determining the appropriate indicators for measuring performance.

5. Collecting the Data

The data will include stakeholders' perceptions of company performance against the criteria they have already helped to formulate as well as relevant data from the company's own management information systems.

6. Writing the Accounts

The accounts and report are produced by the company. This involvement of the organization's own staff reflects the methodology's basis in dialogue between the organization and its stakeholders, and its commitment to learn.

7. Auditing the Accounts

Social accounting carries with it the requirement on the organization to submit its accounts to independent verification.

8. Publication

The accounting statement, approved by the auditor, together with the Auditor's Report are published and distributed to all key stakeholders.

Putting it into Practice

Traidcraft was conscious of the tension that existed between its desire for transparent feedback and the cost of collecting and analysing the required social impact data. In discussions with other more profit-focused businesses, they often made the point that social accounting may be important for 'ethical businesses' like Traidcraft, the Body Shop and the Co-operative Bank, but would be too expensive for them.

Traidcraft addressed the cost issue by developing a system of *social bookkeeping*.[8] Social bookkeeping captures data relevant to the social accounts on a continuous basis through the existing company management accounting systems or by developing new *social* management information systems. The idea was that managers could see how they were doing regularly and make business decisions that took account of the social impact as well as the effect of costs and profits.

A key characteristic of the approach was allowing the stakeholders to make their own observations about the organization's performance and record these in the accounts, and reflect them in the published report. This approach not only limits the scope for misleading statistics and biased accounting, but also enriches the report with a wealth of detailed statistical data and with stakeholders' stories—the real human experience of business.

This information would have little power to change the company unless the social accounts were published. The directors agreed that this was a logical outcome of the methodology and that publication would speed the process of refining the method by encouraging feedback. They recognized that stakeholders would

---

8   C Dey, R Evans and R Gray, 'Towards Social Information Systems and Bookkeeping,' in *The Journal of Applied Accounting Research* (Leicester Business School, 1995).

criticize as well as praise the company, but this too was accepted as necessary for improving performance.

Traidcraft was not interested in compliance but in learning. Rather than seeing social accounting as a threat, the Board, shareholders, staff, customers and suppliers have welcomed it as a unique forum where different stakeholders, many of whom will never meet, communicate with one another about how the company affects their lives.

As these new ways of working emerged so new ways of measuring performance against the combined business and social goals also emerged. The company's commitment to social and ethical accountability required that all changes pass the test of whether they meet stakeholders' expectations in the long term.

The Impact Outside Traidcraft

Traidcraft plc was the first business to develop voluntary social accounts and to publish independently audited reports.

The company recognized that its contribution to fair trade would have only a tiny and localized effect on the problem of poverty. So it was vital to win the hearts and minds of the public to choose justice instead of indifference when they go shopping and to see sacrifice as a virtue rather than the self-indulgence encouraged by advertising and the media.

Traidcraft also sent copies of its Social Accounts to the chief executives of the top 100 companies in the UK. While only a minority responded in those early days, there is a growing interest in what Traidcraft has done and in the idea of corporate social accountability. Not a little credit goes to the business sections and journalists at *The Financial Times*, *The Guardian*, *The Independent* and *The Observer*.

AccountAbility—The Institute and the AA1000 Standard

The Institute of Social and Ethical AccountAbility was established in 1996. In 1999 it published *AA1000, An AccountAbility Framework Standard and Guidelines*. This is a developed version of the original methodology and incorporates the subsequent experience of a wide variety of companies and non-profit organizations practising social accounting around the world.

AA1000's Overarching Principles

Accountability The guiding principle of the whole process is the duty to provide an account of its policies and activities and the impact that they have had, or are likely to have on its stakeholders, and

Inclusiveness The process has to engage all stakeholders in assessing its performance and reflect their perceptions and experiences of the organization fairly.

Principles Relating to the Scope and Nature of the Accounting Process

Completeness The accounting process includes all areas of activity. In addition, it requires an externally verified disclosure of what is included and excluded and the reasons for any exclusions. The organization should be prudent in presenting any adverse impacts of its activities and uncertain outcomes in a balanced manner.

Materiality While stakeholders are engaged in the process of defining what issues and performance indicators are relevant there may be material impacts or performance parameters of which they are not aware. The principle of materiality requires the company to disclose these and the auditors to check that the management systems and reporting are adequate.

Regularity and Timeliness Social and ethical accounts are to be produced regularly so that managers and stakeholders have the relevant information to support decisions they make about the organization. Reports should include information relevant to the accounting period and avoid any that relates to different accounting periods.

Principles Relating to the Meaningfulness of the Information

Comparability The information provided to stakeholders should compare performance over time, against targets set by the company or its external regulators and statutory agencies and against external benchmarks.

Reliability The organization must demonstrate, and the external verifier check, that its information systems are effective, up-to-date and have produced accurate data on the organization's performance.

Accessibility The accounts should be written and communicated in a way that allows all stakeholders to access and understand the information it contains.

Quality Assurance Both the process and the reports should be audited by an independent verifier who will report in any publication of the results on the scope, quality and accuracy of the process and the data.

Principles Governing the Relationship Between Accountability and Management

Embeddedness Accountability must be integrated into the organization's policies, management structures, operations, systems, training and performance measures.

Continuous Improvement The organization must publish targets for improving its performance within reasonable time frames across all key performance indicators and demonstrate appropriate responses to stakeholder concerns and information needs.

The next chapter looks at the theories behind these accountability principles and my own views as a Christian and social accounting practitioner engaged in their development and application.

3
An 'Exegesis' of Accountability

There are a number of parallels between an organization's corporate experience of developing a social account and the Christian experience of salvation:

- the need for conviction—recognizing that laws have been broken and moral and ethical principles transgressed;
- the need for genuine and continuous repentance—turning away from wrong and determining to set and achieve new targets of behaviour;
- acceptance of the possibility, and reality, of forgiveness; and
- the possibility of *perseverance* and renewal.

Such a comparison clearly invites questions about the differences between Christian repentance and re-birth and corporate accountability, transparency and transformation. I would be hesitant about pushing the analogy too far.

Nonetheless, Christians should find much to excite them and much to thank God for, if companies shift away from an instrumental treatment of people and the natural environment in order to maximize profit for shareholders, towards a recognition that people and the environment matter. Social accounting is making a real contribution by exploring the possibility that such changes can be systematically monitored, and by encouraging companies to take on the responsibility for reporting their progress themselves. It is also a shift from an adversarial and exploitative relationship with society to a confessional and servant relationship—in business-speak, disclosure and service.

While the practice of social and ethical accounting happened in advance of any regulatory framework or theoretical program, the process drew from several different theories about social interaction. This chapter outlines the three main current interpretations, which are here termed *emancipation, inclusion* and *managerialist,* and my own theoretical perspective, under the heading *accountability and complexity.*

1. Emancipation: There is More to a Company than its Shareholders

I outlined in chapter one the necessity of seeing business as an integral part of what defines modern society. I also described the concept of *stakeholders* in business activity and the logical extension of this idea to corporate *accountability* to stakeholders. Chapter two described how the social and ethical accounting process evolved in Traidcraft from the principle, set out in its Articles of Association, that the company was *a community of purpose.*

Traidcraft's Foundation Principles drew their inspiration from liberation theology. The activities of the company were intended to incarnate the words and spirit of Jesus when he announced his mission in the synagogue at Nazareth:

The spirit of the Lord is on me,
for he has anointed me
to bring the good news to the afflicted.
He has sent me to proclaim liberty to captives,
sight to the blind,
to let the oppressed go free,
to proclaim a year of favour from the Lord.   (Luke 4.18)

Chris Rowland has written, 'Liberation theology is above all a way of *doing* theology…In many respects [it] harks back to the theological method of an earlier age, when worship, service to humanity and theological reflection were more closely integrated and when the conduct of the Christian life was an indispensable context for theological reflection. What has been rediscovered is the commitment to the poor and marginalized as a determining moment for theology…'[9]

Traidcraft wanted to know what Jesus' statement at Nazareth meant for it and for business generally. Traidcraft's partners were marginalized people in Asia, Africa and Latin America whose poverty, to a large measure, had its roots in the history and contemporary activities of international trade and in the unjust structures that prevented them gaining access to the rich markets of the North. We shared the frustration expressed by the theologian Mary Grey:

> We who tell the story are now positioned in a culture where truth is delivered in media sound-bites, and where the profundity of the Gospel stories of suffering, the suffering of the bodies of poor people are simply not heard, because the implications of hearing are unacceptable in a 'culture of contentment.'[10]

I have earlier used the term 'emancipation' for this theme in social and ethical accounting. Traidcraft's goal was no less than the emancipation of the poor in developing countries from the shackles of unjust and impoverishing international trading relationships and structures. Our method was to run an effective business operation that would 'regard all commercial decisions, processes and structures as stemming from the ethical and practical framework for love in action to be found in the life of Jesus Christ' (Traidcraft's Objectives).

The social accounts were a deliberate attempt to construct a framework within which the company would be made accountable to its partners for carrying out these objectives. While the initial focus of emancipation was Traidcraft's overseas producers, it was quickly realized that a community of purpose embracing all its stakeholders required accountability to them all. So we incorporated appropriate indicators (of change) into our social accounting process.

Traidcraft's impact was always going to be tiny. Changing international trading structures and mainstream business conduct meant finding a more accessible

---

9   C Rowland, (ed), *The Cambridge Companion to Liberation Theology* (Cambridge University Press, 1999) p 3 Introduction.
10   M Grey, *The Shaking of the Foundations—Again! Is there a Future for Christian Theology?* (Cambridge: Von Hügel Institute, St Edmunds College, 1994).

language outside our Christian faith perspective. We found our language in the radical critique of financial accountancy.[11] The basis was an adaptation of the standard Principle-Agency Theory of accounting but extended to include accountability for the different types of capital invested by all stakeholders and accountability for all outcomes, not just financial profit and growth. Stakeholders were to be 'emancipated' by providing information about its activities that they, the stakeholders, regarded as necessary for them to make informed decisions about their relationship with the company.

The essential difference between this view of social accounting and the theories that follow is the community of purpose and the commitment to economic justice. The company is constructed around a set of guiding principles to which its members subscribe and against which its performance is assessed. In the language of postmodernity the validity of what it does has to be determined within its cultural and mission perspective, even when its stakeholders view it from their own, and perhaps other, perspectives. It is within the culture that is shared, the common purpose, that the accountability takes place. It is also a view that regards gross inequality as a fundamental denial of human rights, and of God's law, that we are duty-bound to change through sharing in the struggle of the oppressed.

2. Inclusion: There is More to Corporate Life than Making Profits

Social accountability has drawn much inspiration from the environmental movement, feminism and postmodernism. Here the location of the discussion is less in 'modern' theories of agency, responsibility and accounting, for organizations explicitly defined by their business purpose and internal values, or in liberation, and more in notions of stakeholder dialogue drawn from Jürgen Habermas's idea of the ideal speech situation and discourse ethics. It is consensus among all the legitimate stakeholders that makes a decision or action ethical.

Grey *et al* describe the process thus: 'The approach is built around stakeholder dialogue and its essence lies in providing each of the stakeholders with a voice in the organization. The social account comprises predominantly (but not exclusively) a reporting of the voices of the stakeholders.'[12] Providing a voice sounds pretty similar to the idea of emancipating stake-holders outlined above. But discourse ethics makes no presuppositions about right and wrong—the morality of decisions is determined by the process. This attempt at consense may not prove an effective route to redistributing power and eco-justice.

Some practitioners have taken the importance of stakeholder interaction with the organization beyond dialogue to a point where through successive iterations of the process, the stakeholders, in effect, define the organization and its values. Grey goes on to quote Innes, Nixon and Tagoe,[13] 'the organizational stakeholders

---

11 See Grey, Owen and Adams (1996).
12 R Grey, C Dey, D Owen, R Evans and S Zadek, 'Struggling with the Praxis of Social Accounting' in *Accounting, Auditing and Accountability Journal*, 10/3, (1997).
13 J Innes, W A Nixon and N Tagoe, *Accounting and Strategic Process—A Case Study* (University of Dundee: Discussion Paper ACC/9601, 1996).

are seen as constituting and sustaining their own reality—and that of the organization—both socially and symbolically.'

Even the largest and most powerful of corporations would increasingly concur with the words of Robert Burns,

> O wad some Pow'r the giftie gie us
> To see oursels as others see us!
> It wad frae mony a blunder free us,
> And foolish notion. (To a Louse)

But the degree of stakeholder engagement implied by this theory of social accounting, and the consequent threat to managers' and shareholders' control of the business, is uncomfortable, to say the least, and has led to the third approach which we will examine below.

Christians can learn much from its distinctly postmodern and feminist ring. But difficulties arise with the central notion that the only valid truth is negotiated rather than ontological and appropriated by the individual, in the case of Christians through faith in practice.

For Traidcraft, with its Christian Foundation Principles, the conflict is obvious. But my observation is that the managers, and ideally employees, in many businesses believe passionately in the mission and values of their company and will often articulate them in language that speaks of their 'faith' in the contribution they are making to society. The notion of the company as a community of purpose goes some way to circumventing this difficulty, but only if the idea of a clear functional mission and moral values which stakeholders buy into is upheld.

The other potential conflict for Christians is between our belief in our creatureship and personal responsibility to obey God, love our neighbour and care for creation and the tendency of discourse ethics to lead towards relativism and the denial of individual personal responsibility.

There is no conflict with the central practice of this approach to social accountability, namely that all stakeholders should be involved in determining the performance criteria that will be used to measure the extent to which the organization is following its mission and living its values. Where it begins to depart quite radically from the emancipation theory, or a more conventional view of accountability, is that it fails ultimately to answer the question 'Why?' Why is some behaviour inappropriate, and morally wrong?

Giving stakeholders a voice may lead to moral uncertainty—if the responsibility for corporate ethics ultimately lies with them. Lowest common denominators rarely produce demanding goals. And having a voice does not necessarily lead to emancipation—it may simply give the company better information on which to base its strategies for managing stakeholders. This leads us to the third approach.

3. The Managerialist Approach: Nice Companies Make Profits

The third approach claims no theoretical basis but follows a pragmatic argument. Businesses that have a clear success model and build co-operative and transparent relationships with key partners will be the most successful in the long term. A sort of prosperity gospel for guilt-stricken corporations, but generally described more positively as the 'business case.' Evidence from the Dow Jones Sustainability Index, research by the Tomorrow's Company project in the UK, and the growth in ethical investment funds suggests this is true. And we should not be surprised or cynical.

However, it is has been called a 'managerialist' approach and it has limited emphasis on accountability and justice. Its supporters advocate social accounting in terms of reputation and risk management, which fits nicely with the 'modern,' 'scientific' approach to management and our post-Thatcher capitalist economy. Researchers at Sheffield University have said, 'It could be argued that this *managerialist* perspective has increasingly become the core value of contemporary social audit, that is, the potential for social audit to strengthen and enhance an organization's strategic management procedures. Prominent among the purported benefits are the identification of weaknesses in management control of high-risk activities, and enhanced stability, which enables an organization to mitigate against unexpected shocks.'[14]

There are all sorts of practical ways the managerialist approach limits accountability, stakeholder dialogue and transparency. It is visible in the extent to which some reporting companies have weakened or eliminated stakeholders' involvement in determining performance criteria. Again, companies may rupture the ideal speech situation by restricting the scope of the process to their own limited selection of stakeholders, or by reporting on different stakeholders' perspectives in different accounting periods and reports. Ideally, all stakeholders should have a voice, and hear other stakeholders' voices, evaluating performance relating to the same accounting period and activities.

There is also the issue of audit or verification. It is not surprising, in a rapidly evolving discipline, that conflicting theoretical approaches lead to very different demands being made on the reporting companies by their 'auditors.' Those using a strict rules-based method, using principles developed in financial auditing, are accused of falling into the same analytical myopia as financial accounting. On the other hand, the postmodern approach of stakeholder engagement in verification raises problems with conflicts of interest and with the ability of stakeholders to know what is happening and whether the company's report gives a truthful, complete and balanced view.

From a Christian perspective there are two issues. Firstly, does an organization have the right to use people instrumentally for its own interests? Should it

---

14 D Owen, T A Swift, C Humphrey and M Bowerman, *The New Social Audits: Accountability, Managerial Capture or the Agenda of Social Champions* (Sheffield University, 1999).

manipulate and manage them, and the information they are given, to ensure compliance with an agenda they have little or no part in determining? The answer both for democracy and the kingdom of heaven has to be 'No!'

Secondly, is business capable of defining what being a good neighbour entails? Individuals cannot, because of sin, and companies will be more interested in reputation management than exposure. It is hard to see how a corporation prioritising self interest can in any sense be trusted, or even expected, to give an honest account of its behaviour and its impact on those it affects.

Social accounting has to build trust within the organization and with its stakeholders. Corporate behaviour, even in our caring, stakeholder society, has continued to undermine any residue of trust the majority of disempowered stakeholders once had. Effective, independent audit of the company's processes, impacts and the embeddedness of the accountability concept in its values, behaviour and strategies may be uncomfortable, but I can see little justification for some of the softer approaches involving stakeholder panels or process endorsements by 'the great and the good.'

Repentance can only follow a full recognition of wrongdoing. Most of us need to learn how to tell the difference between right and wrong before we recognize it in our own behaviour. However, the auditor's job is not to make judgments or apportion blame. It is to assure the stakeholders, and other readers, that the organization has been truthful, has an adequate process for 'heart-searching' about the rights and wrongs of its behaviour, and has neither concealed its failings or unfairly promoted its virtues, and that it has given credible assurances of improvement. Independent verification should expose the managerialist approach for its failure to follow the principles of social accountability such as inclusiveness, comprehensiveness and materiality. In practice it has not always done so.

4. *Accountability and Complexity*

The fourth theoretical approach is the author's own, first presented at a seminar on 'Managing Sustainability Dilemmas in the Third World.'[15] It is a view that rejects the classical economic theory of the role of business with its reductionist financial analysis and failure to account for so called 'externalities' such as social, moral and environmental effects. It also attempts to define social and ethical accounting in the general context of sustainability and a 'postmodern,' scientific understanding of complexity.

The old business management paradigms maintained that successful businesses survived by gaining a strategic competitive advantage—product differentiation or cost reduction—or through charismatic leadership by the CEO (chief executive officer). The market theories on which they were based were analytical and reductionist. *Auditing the Market* recognized the scale and efficiency of the

---

15 R Evans 'Social and Environmental Accounting: A Way Out' in Smith, J (ed), *Managing Sustainability Dilemmas in the Developing World* (Cambridge: University of Cambridge Committee for Interdisciplinary Environmental Studies, 1997).

market economy but also its failings. It started with the assertion that while the market 'copes efficiently with billions of transactions daily, its permissive and amoral operation takes little or no account of the social and environmental consequences of the market process and its impact on individual human lives.' The paper went on to argue for businesses to fill this ethical role voluntarily by adopting regular and systematic, social accounting procedures. While voluntarism works for the socially responsible company, a stronger argument, based on some first principles, is needed to extend the reach of accountability.

If we think of the company as the sum of its people, activities and goals, its functioning can be seen as a complex system of interactions based on prescribed and emerging patterns of behaviour. But it is not self-contained—it is one organization living in a set of comparable entities within a wider social and environmental system.

A general systems theory approach would define the company in terms of its relationship with a complex system involving suppliers, competitors, customers, the civic, human, and bio-physical environment and other agents in the system in which it operates. Such an understanding of business would free the discussion from the difficulties of agreeing a basis for ethical judgment by focussing attention on system behaviour rather than individual morality. It also deals with the obvious, and obviously absurd, reductionism of divorcing business from its human and social origins and treating it as a purely economic function.

The importance of these wider interactions is more apparent today than ever before in such modern phenomena as real-time information exchange, sophisticated marketing tools like bar codes and 'electronic point-of-sale' data links (EPOS), increased environmental awareness and the globalisation of consumer and capital markets. Managers today are required to monitor the effects of more and more of these interactions. Large systems of interacting agents cannot be described and understood by traditional linear processes of analysis and deterministic prediction. Business needs a new management paradigm that recognizes the import of increased interaction and globalisation.

For the last thirty years business schools and management gurus have swung back and forth between two principal paradigms of business management—the strategic management paradigm and the leadership paradigm. The former has often proved to be too narrowly focused, too static and unrealistically inflexible while the latter is too susceptible to fashion and inimical to rational explanation. Both function by subordinating everything to the strategy or the leader, effectively reducing other agencies at work in the system to instruments of the prime mover.

Researchers in disciplines as diverse as genetics, artificial intelligence, neurology, geology, cellular biology, quantum mechanics and economics have been talking to each other about a new way of looking at their different 'worlds.' Dissatisfied with the traditional approach of analysing individual events they looked at the complexity of many agents and events co-operating and competing in the vast and complex systems, which they form in the real world. These scientist are beginning to discover how the systems they study live and die, create and evolve new events and things, and even aggregate into new systems.[16]

Business cannot be managed effectively, or in a way that adds to the common wealth, by algorithms and heuristics alone, or by imaginative scenario planning, or by relying on the ethics of its founders or managers. We have to recognize that businesses are systemically linked with economic, political, social, spiritual, environmental, information and communications systems. We have to start discovering how they actually interact and evolve now, if we are to have any idea about where business is going in the future.

We can start at the micro level by looking at the interactions within the company and between the company and its human, economic and physical and biological environment. That is what a social account of a business is intended to do.

The objectives, mission statement and values of the company are like the DNA in the cells of an organism. The DNA reacts with the chemicals in its environment and replicates itself into new strands of DNA, which in turn can form new protein molecules. They in turn create new cells, organisms and 'societies.' The real objectives of a company, which may not be identical to the stated objectives and will always be complex, will inform the way the organization behaves and the impact it has on people who are involved in it, and on its environment.

If we want to know how businesses will survive we need to observe their interactions with their environment and to see how feedback can enable the company to enhance its fitness to survive. What for instance are the boundary conditions between unrestricted competition (chaos) and co-operation (order)? Can the system 'outwit' agencies controlling scarce resources within it by adapting its requirements to substitute resources? For example, will capital always determine fitness to survive, making the system apparently subservient to the needs of the providers of capital, or will other factors acquire the greater significance in future?

Social accounting has attempted to address the most serious question facing business in the 21st century. How can human society, now largely integrated by communications and global environmental effects, survive when the economic system, dominated by business, is in such extreme imbalance?

This *systems* approach challenges the historic myopia of Christians about business, corporate responsibility and personal faith. It also challenges Christian indifference to the natural world, at least in the Protestant tradition since the Reformation. It offers a model for integrating a truly biblical understanding of society with a contemporary scientific understanding of the natural world and its complex interacting systems.

As a footnote to this discussion I would point readers to the writings of Danah Zohar and Ian Marshall.[17] Their basic thesis is that, underlying the complexity of

---

16   See M M Waldorp, *Complexity—The Emerging Science at the Edge of Order and Chaos* (Simon and Schuster, 1992).
17   Zohar, D and Marshall, I (1991) *The Quantum Self* and (1994) *The Quantum Society* (London: Flamingo).

the natural and physical world, quantum mechanics provides an integrating system of physical reality. It explains the uncertainty, and therefore potentiality, of events at the atomic level and the interconnectedness of all events. Their books explain how the understanding of reality provided by quantum mechanics can provide a model for the potentiality of individual personal development and social development and the underlying connectedness of action and consequence. If the model is valid it finally undermines the libertarian thesis that humans can act in their own interests without affecting others. This truth is at the heart of the Christian belief that God created and sustains all things and Jesus' message that we are not only responsible for ourselves before God, but also for our neighbours.

Danah Zohar speculates about God 'as something embodied within, or something which uses, the laws of physics,' who is identified with 'the basic sense of direction in the unfolding universe—even, perhaps, with an evolving consciousness within the universe…involved at every moment in a mutually creative dialogue with his world.' She also suggests that 'the basic drive towards greater ordered coherence might be seen as the physical basis of Grace, that which allows us, through relationship, to transcend our individuality (The Fall) and return to unity (God). For Christians the saving relationship is the Body of Christ.' Perhaps Paul was inspired with a similar breadth of understanding when he wrote

> He is the image of the unseen God,
> the first-born of all creation,
> for in him were created all things
> in heaven and on earth:
> everything visible and invisible…
> and in him all things hold together…
> God wanted all fullness to be found in him
> and through him to reconcile all things to him…   (Colossians 1.15–20)

As a Christian I have struggled, since school days, with the apparent conflict between faith's creation perspective and science. I find these new non-Newtonian pictures of reality as complex, interrelated systems at the macro and social level, supported by a universal system of principles embodying potentiality (a new heaven and a new earth!) and interconnectedness at the fundamental physical level, consistent with my understanding of the Bible. They are also deeply satisfying.

Conclusions

In describing these different theoretical approaches to social and ethical accounting it is not my intention to suggest that any one is sufficient on its own and the others wrong or redundant. In practice we draw on the strengths of each. The point of differentiating them is to warn readers of the dangers of reductionism while emphasizing that the quest for a coherent theoretical approach is important. It may make the difference between social and ethical accounting being a short-lived fashion in business and it becoming a tool for real change and business taking a greater responsibility for people and planet and the pursuit of justice.

The search for a coherent Christian perspective on economics and business practice, an alternative to free market economics, is one in which Christians are obliged to engage. We are in the world and can only *choose* to ignore the issues, not to avoid them. The growing practice of social accountability in business is an exciting opportunity to engage at the practical level, with our life decisions, as well as the theoretical level, with our minds and our faith.

While my fellow practitioners in social accounting may find my analysis strays well beyond the pragmatic business case for doing it, I hope my fellow Christians will see how this exciting phenomenon can help them bring their values and their message of the kingdom into the sphere of business accountability. If you do, then please go out into all the world and support its promotion and extension.

Appendix
The Reports, Organizations and Further Reading

As a practising social accountant and auditor, and a director of the Institute of Social and Ethical AccountAbility, it would be inappropriate for me to comment on particular examples of social accounts that have been published. I hope the explanation of the process and of my understanding of the beliefs and values driving its development and use will act as a guide for those who want to know more. You will have to make your own judgments about the quality of the reports and the companies producing them.

The list below includes most of the companies who have produced reports to date, which broadly follow the principles described in this booklet. Most will be available to view on their web-sites or you can ask the companies to send you reports by mail.

A good place to start is with the 2000 Social Reporting Award winners: The Co-operative Bank, Shell International, United Utilities and Traidcraft. By the time you read this there will be more. Find out from the AccountAbility, ACCA and GRI web-sites listed below.

The Body Shop International, www.bodyshop.co.uk
Bristol-Myers Squibb, www.bms.com
British Airports Authority, www.baa.co.uk
BP Amoco, www.bpamoco.com
BT, www.bt.com

Camelot, www.camelotplc.com
The Co-operative Bank, www.co-operativebank.co.uk
CWS, www.co-op.co.uk
NatWest Bank, www.natwestgroup.com
Novo Nordisk, www.novo.dk
Proctor & Gamble, www.pg.com/99sr
Railtrack, www.railtrack.co.uk
Rio Tinto , www.riotinto.co.uk
Shell International, www.shell.com
South African Breweries, www.sab.co.za
Southern Sun, www.southernsun.com
Traidcraft, www.traidcraft.co.uk
Triple Trust Organization, www.tto.org.za
TXU—Eastern Group, www.eastern.co.uk
United Utilities, www.unitedutilities.com
Van City Savings and Credit Union, www.vancity.com

Organizations

Institute of Social and Ethical AccountAbility, www.accountability.org.uk
Global Reporting Initiative, www.globalreporting.org
ACCA (for Social Reporting Awards), www.accaglobal.com
CSEAR (Centre for Social and Environmental Accounting Research) www.gla.ac.uk/Acad/accounting/csear
New Economics Foundation, www.neweconomics.org
Traidcraft, www.traidcraft.co.uk

Further Reading

R Adams, *Who Profits?—The Traidcraft Story* (Oxford: Lion 1989)
R Grey, D Owen, C Adams, *Accounting and Accountability* (London: Prentice Hall, 1996)
R Higginson, *Called to Account* (Guildford: Eagle 1993)
P Johnson and C Sugden, *Markets, Fair Trade and the Kingdom of God* (Regnum Books, 2000)
S Robinson, *Serving Society: The Social Responsibility of Business* (Grove Ethics booklet E 86)
J Webley, *Can Companies Sin?* (Grove Ethics booklet E 85)
S Zadek, P Pruzan, R Evans (eds), *Building Corporate Accountability* (London: Earthscan, 1997)

BT has published a useful series of Occasional Papers on the role of business in a sustainable society. See the BT web-site for details.